FAST ASLEEP
IN TERRAPIN
S O U P

POEMS OF LOVE, GRIEF, AND OTHER NONSENSE

LJ O'HAGAN

First paperback edition 2025
Via ORIGAMI PLATYPUS
Book design by LJ O'Hagan

ORIGAMI PLATYPUS

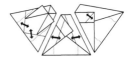

ISBN 978 1 3999 8943 5
(Paperback)

Contact: ljohaganwords@outlook.com

For *you*.

INNARDS.

INNARDS.

INNARDS.

READY, ABLE

A C K N O W L E D G E M E N T S

I'M NOT HERE
THIS ISN'T
HAPPENING

CLARENCE.

My imaginary friend thinks I'm imaginary. I usually find him in the garden, pissing about with the gnomes. Apparently, when I go back in the house, he makes dinner, watches Netflix, and just generally chills out. My imaginary friend has six fuzzy arms, is covered in periwinkle fur, and has a great big bulbous nose that dangles past his top lip. "You haven't got a TV or a kitchen!" He just shrugs his shoulders and replies, "Can't see yours either." I asked him why nobody else looks like him and everybody else looks like me? He told me he'd imagined us all and that he actually had lots of other imaginary friends. I tried to un-imagine him, no luck. He slammed the garden shed door and I vanished into thin air.

HATMAN.

Hatman's hat blew off. It passed a couple of ducks and koi carp, a swordfish and a pod of dolphins. His hat passed whales and narwhals, a devilfish and those ones with the lamps on their heads. It tumbled through the abandoned alleyways of Atlantis and briefly got tangled up in a family of viper dogfish. Eventually, Hatman's hat scuttled past the feet of Poseidon, who forked it with his trident and added it to his collection. Hatman looked around all the charity shops but couldn't find anything with the same kind of feather on it.

DOVETAIL.

"I'm gonna marry you"
I predicted to a stranger. She
nodded and told me she already
knew. We nodded at each other
and shook on it. Then, we went our
separate ways to wait it out.

ACTOR.

I got the lead part! I wasn't sure how, as I'd never auditioned for the role, nor had I ever acted in or auditioned for anything, ever. Sure enough, the letter arrived. I wondered what this part could be for, who I'd be playing, and who would be my supporting cast? I scoured the letter from top to bottom for more information - a contact number, email, anything. A quick message in the group chat to let the lads know that this guy had made the big time, that it was now likely I'd be making new friends of a much higher calibre and prestige. I hired an agent and took a trip to the sunbeds. I arranged a film crew to document my process.

EASY MEAT.

The drawings from my sketchbook came to life. They were all impeccably handsome and muscular; each scribble had incredible posture. I took an eraser to these tiny little stud muffins and watched their shoulders slump.

THE SEER.

The seer was draped in black, with eyes absent from the pale skin where a face once was. Obsidian juice dripped from its gaping mouth, drooling and drying around its chin. It fumbled some sticks on the ground, spat into a ramekin, and predicted my death. The seer waggled its deceased, peeled fingers in my face and said something about the prophecy being bulletproof. I told the creep I wasn't buying it. "I ain't going anywhere." The seer creaked its skull 90° and groaned widely. The eerie cunt clacked on about "The prophecy, the prophecy." I gathered my rucksack and got on with enjoying the other attractions around Centre Parcs.

TOOTHACHE.

A couple of teeth fell out first, followed by a pair of rattlesnake eggs. My lips tore as I vomited out a fire hydrant and several mystic jewels. An inflatable alligator jostled through my jaws, onto the ever growing pile of tat. My head exploded into a museum of total nonsense.

UNDIES.

A stranger pushed me directly into Victoria's Secret. The lad working there then pushed me into a rail full of black lacy lingerie. I fell directly through the straps of a mesh bra and matching knickers. Leaning my debit card onto the card reader for stability, the cashier nudged me back out into the shopping centre and wished me a good day.

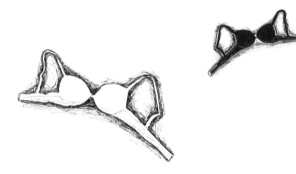

INTIMACY.

Sketching you naked and
I've drawn a funny nose.

TETE-A-TETE.

My doppelgänger replied to my spare room ad, this boy's name was Wyatt. According to his profile, he enjoyed hiking *(nope)*, watching the F1 *(snooze)*, and reading true crime *(weirdo)*. He arrived with a bottle of rosé, *(yuck)*. I offered Wyatt some Ferrero Roche. He declined, raising one hand and wincing. We sat in the kitchen, trying to find anything we had in common. Nothing. I asked Wyatt what date he was looking to move in. He yawned, scratched his chin, and told me he wasn't really looking to move out of his place. "Why are you here then?" I puzzled. "B e c a u s e   y o u ' r e   m y   d o p p e l g ä n g e r." Silence hung for the next twenty five minutes as we tucked into our respective wine and chocolates.

ROASTED.

I opened a cafè where the staff could only answer "no." The flaws in the rule became clear through week one. Unfortunately, I had hired an unbelievable team. Customers stopped coming, and the cafè went to total shit. After months of failed business, I burned the place down. Whoops. My phone was blowing up the next morning - friends, family, the fire department, and the fuzz. I trudged down to the ruins of my coffee shop. When I got there, I found my team floating around the rubble, refusing to help.

COLOSSUS.

My fiancé transformed into a squid. I became an overnight expert in marine biology to gain a better understanding of her new, complex nature. She wouldn't often be in the mood to flirt or watch movies, but did still enjoy her favourite, Stella Artois. I splashed a pint over her mantle and nuzzled inside her reluctant tentacles. Her colossal eye loomed over me as I surfed the forums for data.

STRIKER.

       "Today, I'm gonna play
s   t   r   i   k   e   r!"
I woke up excited. I grabbed my
boots from the cupboard and ran
downstairs to give them a scrub. I
was filled to the brim with
adrenaline. I told my partner the
news, "I've got a good feeling about
it!" She told me to stick to what I
know, handing me my whistle and
yellow cards.

CATAPULT.

The fur ball arrived. He sat in the middle of the lounge, and we stared at him intensely. He stretched and purred and slinked off into the bedroom to rub his anus on the carpet. We sat cross-legged on the rug, waiting for him to come back and break the silence.

FAKE PLASTIC CHEESE.

                The phone keeps ringing,
over and over. I gnaw open a third
slice of cheese. I climb inside, shut
the door firmly behind me, and
crawl through to the back of the
fridge, making my home among
forgotten,

                vigorous

                                islands

        of

                        mushrooms

            and

                            pesto.

I'm sprouting tendrils by my fifth
slice of cheese. The call would wait.

HIDE AND SEEK.

       I painted myself in pastel
pink and nailed a frame to my
f   o   r   e   h   e   a   d.
I clutched onto a vase, stood as still
as possible, and waited for you to
get home.

THE LEFT HANDED GIANT.

Rambling down the mountain came the giant. He'd been away for a while, but now he was back, bearing gifts. He hauled a sack from over his shoulder and poured the contents on top of his crush. Her spine was broken and her face caved in, her guts splattered across the pavement. He poked and flicked and grunted at her limp body. The gifts were great, but they were just too big; this giant couldn't seem to ever get it right.

DAISY.

I asked Daisy if she loved me, but she ran out of petals before she could answer.

CRASH BANDICOOT.

Bunkered down deep beneath the soil, our days became entwined, where time couldn't find us. Thunderclaps buried the noise of our turbulent lives, twisting wildly away. We met during the storm and found shelter together while the lightning struck. Once the rainclouds passed, the rumbling of unopened boxes came c r a s h i n g   b a c k   i n t o e   a   r   s   h   o   t.

SHADOW PUPPETS.

Our train is taking us home as the sky sweeps from watermelon to lazuli. Neither of us know yet that this is our one last good day.

Our train judders along. All that's left to do is to rest our heads on each other's shoulders.

WON'T STOP TURNING UNTIL I'M TWISTED

DEEP SEA DIVER.

You asked me to jump first
into the deep blue sea. I swam
through the coral and clams,
weaving between seaweed and
l u m i n o u s   p l a n k t o n.
Your feet dangled and rippled
above the surface. I dove further
and further down to the depths,
where the fish have fangs. You
asked me to jump first, and I did it.

GUT FEELING.

Cats were speaking human now. Naturally, I got chatting to the big guy. I asked him his thoughts on the vibe in the flat, what he thought was going on? He c h i r r u p e d, "it is what it is." He sat on my lap and sulked. We both knew what was coming.

RAPUNZEL, RAPUNZEL.

Submerged in sludge at the
bottom of a pit each morning, the
grime congealed between her eyes.
I plunged my arms into the mud
and dug, trying to grasp her hand.
The bog bubbled beneath us as I
sank into the swamp, fading into
m   u   c   k.

MIMIC.

We taught the parrot all the worst swear words. It turns out he knew most of them already. He actually had quite a bit to say about the pair of us.

MINOTAUR.

I'd woken up **MAD!**
I bulldozed through my door frame
and tumbled into the landing.
Bubbling from the volcanic
floorboards, I charged down the
stairs to charge down some eggs on
toast - which, I charged
the fuck out of by the way.
N O F U C K I N G A B O U T!
I charged out of the house and into
the street, darting my rabid eyes
left to right, pawing the ground
beneath me. Drool and eggs
evacuating my chops as I roared in
anguish. I charged all the way to the
coast and dived far out to sea.

SHOPPER.

This leopard was lost. Hogging the Pringles and nibbling at torn-apart packs of Gouda, I thumped my trolley into the beast's back legs. Its spots glowed at the sight of my six-pack of Cherry Bakewell. I followed it to the self-scanners and watched it struggle with the bagging area.

ICEBERG.

"I fuckin' told you cunts!"

Gargled

the drowning

chef garde-manger.

ᑲՈB.

       Tentatively wandering into the middle of the boozer, minding my way of the wooden chandelier and glass beams. Tables, chairs, the bar, and all the staff clung to the ceiling. Everything and everyone in this pub was upside down. Folk stared down/up at me like I was the lunatic, cluelessly lurking around above/below them. Tryna make head or tail of the specials board, I made my way back out the door and tumbled 40 feet to the curb.

SCREECHER.

A law had been passed that required everyone to speak at a controlled volume in public. Anything up to the length of a six-person table was fair game. If you breached the next table, you'd be executed on the spot. Pubs and cafès were infested with executioners, clad in butter-yellow bodysuits and blacked-out reflective masks. They carried AK-47s, which, to be honest, shut most of us up. The first to go were the screechers. Attention seekers were lined up and annihilated. The population nosedived by 40%, making it so much easier to get a table anywhere. Due to the lack of custom across the country, noise levels were able to increase. Tables of eight were now quietly debating who would be next to face the wall.

THE HARE AND THE PEA.

"There's a hare in my bowl!" The waiter apologised but didn't quite grasp my complaint. He explained how unfortunate this sort of thing was and offered 50% off our bill. "You're not getting it. There's a *hare* in my broth!" The spritely critter sprang from our table and cannonballed into a nearby leek and pea soup. Apparently, the hare belonged to the owner and sort of ran the roost around this restaurant. The kitchen doors swung wildly in the distance as the hare caused havoc for the chef de partie.

HOTDOGS.

"Tighter, tighter!" **HONK!** **HONK!** "Wrap them tighter!" These guys were the worst. The ludicrous cunts had wrapped the entire audience in pigskin, blowing sage and peppercorns through a horn and into our faces. The ringmaster sharpened his knives, balancing one foot on a beach ball. A group of three short arses performed backflips throughout the Big Top. **H O N K! H O N K!** Sections of the audience were still gawping and clapping beneath their constricting pigskin cocoons. The brutish jesters began to wheel us towards the ring of fire, poking pitchforks into our bottoms.

LODGER.

I released an alligator into
the   flat. I   rustled   around
q   i   t   y
   u   e   l
grabbing snacks whenever it fell
asleep.

MAGNETS.

"W h e r e   a r e   y o u?"
She gripped my hand, resting
her   forehead   against   mine.
My iris shifted from grey to green.
She   squinted   and   smirked   in
that   way   only   she   could.
"W h e r e   d o   y o u   g o   t o?"

KIMONO.

Soaked copper hair draped over emerald shoulders. She sat on the floor between my legs, her cheek against my knee. I held my breath, hoarding every second we had.

SPORES.

You're always sad.
I'm always sad.

I've been breathing it in.
You've been breathing it in.

Now I'm sick.
Now you're sick.

41.

MURMURATIONS.

Grayson emerged from his shell, having split himself into tiny particles that contorted between different shapes and sizes. He swooped and swirled through the aquarium, hoping his new appearance would lift Lily's sombre spirit. Lily knew Grayson was still in there somewhere, inside the spiralling cloud. He was now just broken and swarming, trying too hard. She turned her head away from Grayson's kiss and clawed her way into the sand.

PINNED.

"Oheh eh hukeh oor!"
I dribbled out onto the floor.
As my tongue pulsated
on the other side of the door.

ECHO CHAMBER.

"Y o u ' r e   n o t
l i s t e n i n g!"
she groaned, chopping off my head.
My   formerly   attached   skull,
haircut, face, and mind rolled down
the corridor. I memorised the walls
and imagined all the colours we'd
planned to paint them.

DIM SUM.

Our fingers fluttered blindly, invading the nearest oyster pail. A lucky dip of char siu dumplings, vegetable gyoza and rice noodle rolls packed with shrimp or beef. We lay like mirrored chalk sketches fused together, my palm resting faintly on your toes. Out of all the words we had access to, why couldn't either of us think of a single one of them to say?

BENSON.

The cat learned to wink.

I hated it.

He had already taken up smoking
menthol cigarettes;
now this shit.

PLEASE DON'T
TAKE THIS
FEELING
I HAVE FOUND
AT LAST

LEMON.

They were making you
r a d i o a c t i v e,
at least for a little while.
Strapped down inside the
quarantine zone, doors boarded up.
I wriggled into my hazmat suit
and began the ascent. Patients
peeked through apertures from
within their chambers. Patrolling
helicopters, blind to my voyage and
concealed in the clouds. A lemon
glow encased you. We lay on the
hospital bed together and planned
o u r   e n t i r e   f u t u r e.

MENU.

"**More jelly!**" I couldn't believe chef was asking for more jelly - 90% of the menu was already jelly substitutes. Jelly pork belly with delicious orange jelly jus. Jelly udon noodles in a hot jelly broth. We'd just added croque monsieur for lunch time, which was made of jelly. Chef was carrying a gigantic tray of jelly carrots, she was taking on the roast. Jelly parsnips and Yorkshire puds all but confirmed it. I took a shot of jelly vodka and got to work on gravy.

GLUE.

        "Glue my face to yours?!"
You   explained   again   that
you just needed some space.
"Nose to nose or cheek to cheek?
Let's   g o   g o   g o!"

MASTERPIECE.

On my first day at ceramics class, I'd made a masterpiece. A natural. The novices looked on in awe as my magnificent lump of clay emerged into view. It wasn't just fantastic; it was perhaps the greatest creation the world of ceramics had ever seen. My tutor hissed that this class was for beginners, I insisted that I'd never "thrown clay" in my life! The mood shifted. I began to criticise my creation, pulling it apart, which didn't help my cause. This thing was flawless. My fellow throwers rallied against me, lobbing terracotta bombs as the others held me down on the potter's wheel. Once I was completely covered, these cunts locked me in the kiln and toasted me.

MANOEUVREBOARD.

Limbs ballooned on the first squeeze, tripling in size. Shiny, fleshy blimps swelled from my torso. On the second squeeze, my head inflated. An exhibition of grotesque veins and arteries tunnelled beneath the skin as my face flushed transparent and smooth, my eyes and tongue propelling a yard ahead. The third, fourth and fifth squeeze left my elastic cadaver devoid of any air at all.

51°30'21.1"N 0°09'39.1"W

56.

YOU & I

There   is   a   blue   whale
s   w   i   m   m   i   n   g
in the night sky. Only you and I can
see.

LUNCHBOX.

Am I alive? Am I famous? Am I short? Do I have long hair? Have I been to space? Can you find me on IMDb? Am I fictional? Do I speak? Am I irrational? Can I live forever? Do I grow? Am I painful? Have I been in pain? Have I hurt people? Have I kept people alive? Have I ever let you down? Do I speak more than one language? Do I make bad decisions? Do I act first and think later? Am I chaotic? Am I distant? Do I disappear? Am I unreliable? Do I obsess? Will I still be here tomorrow? Have I lost meaning over time? Do people remember me when I'm gone? Can you find me in small places? Do I feel safe? Am I hard work? Do you recognise me?

Am I love?

труппа.

(TROUPE)

Don't ask how I infiltrated this Russian Beryozka dance troupe, but I'm here. Tripping over my skirt and dropping my birch, I'm all over the place. After the eighth time I tumbled from the stage, I made a beeline for the cloakroom. The girls glided over like a flock of phantoms to calm me down. They were superb. I wiped my nose and dried my eyes on the hem of my skirt. I asked if there was room for one member of the troupe to freestyle? The girls shook their heads, easing my arm into the sleeve of my suede tan bomber.

BOWLING.

A grand piano fell from a fifth-floor balcony and landed on the newlyweds. The good news is that it was made of sponge. The bad news is that their bowl smashed on the curb - and that this couple were g o l d f i s h.

THE NOBODY NEBULA.

Perched on the windowsill, gazing at the glimmering nebula beneath us, nobody knew where we were. Nobody knew us at all. Our tower grazed the planets as we sipped at our lagers. You wrapped yourself around me, pointing out Neptune as I drew your towel away. Supernovas at your back, your calves clutching my shoulders. You loved me, and I loved you, and nobody could find us here.

JUGGLER.

The juggler dropped everything. Toppling ripe tomatoes splattered and extinguished several blazing batons. She tumbled a bunch of tennis balls and throwing knives on top of the expanding mess. Commemorative plates and posh mirrors spilt into shards on the kitchen laminate. The juggler had juggled for three years straight, and now she was exhausted. I teed her up some watermelons and cricket bats, which she tried her best to manoeuvre. I leapt into the cascading objects, hoping the juggler could find a way to juggle me. As she collapsed, I kissed the deck. A roll of armadillos clobbered the backs of our heads, drenched in a dozen duck eggs.

GOBSTOPPER.

Grayson was devastated. Before he could ask why, Lily rammed a gobstopper down his beak. Grayson scratched his head, w h a t   t h e   f u c k   h a s h a p p e n e d   h e r e   t h e n? Lily slid the engagement ring from her claw and knocked it in behind the gobstopper. The dream team was over. Tears rippled down Grayson's dejected mush, flooding the tank with sadness. The pair, buoyed by their carapace, drifted to opposite ends of the aquarium.

SANDCASTLE.

We threw our walls
together, built a fortress, and filled
it with love. We moved ourselves in,
and it crumbled beneath its own
w   e   i   g   h   t.

RICE COOKER.

I got really into the rice cooker. I was adding sesame oil, chocolate chips, all sorts of things to the rice. Each evening, I sat down with a fork and took my time over each and every grain. You mentioned that maybe the rice cooker could do with going away, that we should discuss how we'd divvy up the rest of our possessions.

FORCE MAJEURE.

I flung an anchor through the living room window; it pierced deep into the roadside onyx. Tying the chain around my waist, you handed me our contract, neon lime tracks scrawled across its pages. The typhoon ripped through the flat and carried you away.

Why hadn't I read the small print?

MINE.

        I invited over a new friend and left him in the lounge while I grabbed us some beers. I returned to a jet of urine arching toward my CD collection. This guy was pissing on all of my stuff - the sofa was soaked, curtains were dripping, and the TV wasn't looking as dry as I'd remembered. He turned to face me, still pissing by the way, and popped his chap into one of the bottles of Heineken. We stood, we stared. He declared the word "mine" and went and made a mess of my bookshelf.

EL DORADO.

You told me you hate your
eyes, brown and narrow - a hickory
woodland of muddied footsteps
and broken branches. But you've
never seen your eyes as they're
touched by sunlight, as they pour
like syrup, keyholes to El Dorado's
undiscovered caverns in the dunes.
If only you could see your eyes this
way, you'd no longer yearn for
greens or blues. You'd treasure this
hidden gold within the woods.
You'd understand those trodden
paths weren't people walking
through you, but an audience
arriving, hoping to catch the next
s   u   n   r   i   s   e.

THE TIDE.

Remember
the day I sent
you the ocean?
I captured the waves
just for you,
little crab.

♋.

THE HANDOVER.

Folds barely able to contain themselves beneath strip upon strip of crinkled brown tape. I left the box at the bottom of the stairs for a month, trying my best to ignore it as it bounced around, slamming against the bottom step and skirting board. A deafening squeal clambered out from a small incision in the left flank. The miserable piñata rumbled and burst, flooding the downstairs landing with old t-shirts, Polaroid photos, and love letters. My mint-condition unicorn skull sat deep in the heart of the box, unmoved and unwanted.

WYATT.

Wyatt turned up again, banging on the front door. Fuck's sake. I pried open the bedroom window and shouted down, "H e y t w i n n i e , w h a t d o y o u w a n t n o w?" He'd brought a vintage Monopoly board and was wondering if I was still into the whole doppelgänger thing. Of course, I hated Monopoly, but I let the cunt in anyway; I could tell he needed this.

ALL THE WOLVES HAVE ARRIVED AT YOUR DOOR

USER NOT FOUND.

I was erased.
I scanned the area through
sheer vibe alone to see if I
was somewhere. Not a sniff. I sort
of lingered around formlessly in
the unknown for a bit, gathered
my thoughts and tried not to
take it to heart. Probably
a good reason.

GOOD WEATHER FOR DUCKS.

My bedroom started raining. I flicked up an umbrella as the clouds gathered around my lampshade. It was pissing it down in here. Sparks flew from my television sockets, my belongings pirouetted through the air. Puffing out my cheeks, my appendages flailed. I watched through bloodshot eyes as the last few drops sunk into my new world.

THE COLLECTOR.

       I had been collected, zipped up and vacuum-sealed inside thick, sweaty plastic to keep me in mint condition. I wriggled my eyes from left to right and back to left again, trying to get a look around. The cloaked collector spun on their chair, cackling into the stale air.

IT'S ONLY DANCING.

A shadowed figure twirled across the pavement, street-lights shifting -growing and shrinking, falling behind, reappearing. There wasn't anything I wouldn't do for this shadow. I searched my pockets for a lighter and promised I would keep this shadow safe. But shadows don't fall in love; they belong to someone else. Its owner took a turn, and she followed. I swayed the lighter behind my hand and gripped my own shadow tightly. "It's just you and me now, brother!" His eyes, faint and struggling against the gravel. What had I let happen to him.

OUTLOOK NOT SO GOOD.

"C H O M P!" My bed swallowed me up! With a quick scout around, I found fifteen quid, a few Maltesers, an ex-girlfriend, a treasure map, springs, all of my memories, a copy of *Eternal Sunshine* on DVD, and a magic eight ball. I attempted to reconcile with Roxanne and come up with a plan, but she wasn't interested. I popped the choccies in my gob, loaded my pockets with the cash, and tried to get some kip. I heard Roxanne on her side, leafing through a magazine.

INKED.

I got a tattoo. It spread all over my face and inside my mouth. It made its way down my throat and into my abdomen. The tattoo grew out of my fingertips, covering my arms and chest. The soles of my feet were covered in ink. It crawled up my legs and gorbed my unmentionables. I shaved my head, plucked my teeth, and gouged out my eyes. I wondered how my new look would go down in the staffroom the next day.

MANDELBULB.

"Lily is typing…"
I hover, dull pulses oscillating
inside my whirlpooling stomach. A
low hum slithers beneath my fractal
body. My guts and soul and secrets
and heart feed back and loop
between each other in a constant
flow. "Offline."

FLIRTING.

Glass full of snakes and a lady motioning the cheers sign. I n t e r e s t i n g. I blushed. Without wanting to appear rude, I took my first sip of the snakes. F u c k i n g   r a n k. Inconspicuously emptying the snakes into my palm, I glanced at the lady across the bar and smiled, offering her an appreciative nod. The snakes now biting me inside my clenched fist. One had wrapped around my ring finger, painting my digit a delicious plum. The lady continued to admire me from across the bar as I took another sip from my glass of snakes. Sweat and blood dripped from my eyeballs as I sent over an espresso martini and flashed a final smile. As her cocktail arrived, my head hit the bar. The rest of the snakes gobbled me up.

NUDE.

A nude man sat next to me on a park bench. I avoided eye contact but eventually buckled. "How come you're nude then?" He slapped his thighs and huffed. "Why do you think?" I wasn't entirely sure how this guy's day was going. I asked, "How's your day going?" He landed his head in his hands. "What do you think?" Ah, this guy was going through it.

WASHED UP.

Umpteen cans strapped to my torso, I tumbled out to sea. I dunked my head under, business as usual down there. Slippery blobs squirmed around my little trunks, and suave octopodes juggled pebbles like professionals. Floating on my back, I cracked a can and poured piss-warm lager onto my face. Drifting past the wind farms, I washed up in a small port off the South of France. The locals gathered to lather me in crème solaire as I berated them in my native tongue.

85.

HAPPY BIRTHDAY.

One last gasp of air as the moon crawls to its summit. My bones snap and splinter, tusks pierce my jowls. My face creaks long, my jaw dangles astray. Tendons and ligaments erupt through the skin as my contorting back shatters over and over again. Howling into dusk, I consider leaving a voicemail to wish you all the happiness you could never find with me.

GOBLINS.

Goblins! Goblins! Goblins! This was a goblin wedding. The groom awaited his new bride at the altar, cloaked in nothing but a loincloth and resting a wooden mallet on his shoulder. His groomsmen, smeared in vomit, tucked into a plate of chicken bones, as per tradition. The xylophonist clubbed the teeth from a pig's skull to the tune of 'What a Wonderful World.' We turned in awe. The bride arrived in a stunning squirrel hide, held together with cocktail sticks and staples. The stench was truly unbearable, and we all began to weep. By the time the repulsive couple met, two of the groomsmen had ripped each other's faces off and were wiping down the interior of the abandoned swimming pool.

RITUAL.

Trifle was having a comeback. Every café, bakery and fast food joint worth its weight had trifles coming out their arse. Bars ditched the pints for trifles with a high alcohol content. On Thursday evenings, I'd strip off and lower myself into the bathtub, which I furnished with custard and sherry the night before. I crumbled in sponge alongside pre-made fruit bombs, a midweek ritual. I squirted whipped cream into my mouth directly from the canister.

THE BEDTIME IMP.

Drifting off, I peeked open
an eye and found an imp at the base
of my bed. It had my linen quilt
wrapped around its fists and was
giving it a tug. "What d'ya think
you're doing, mate?!" I yawned,
into its ghastly bog-green grimace.
The imp started cackling, rolling on
the floor, holding its belly and
kicking its feet. I huffed, flipped my
pillow over to the cold side, and
repositioned myself facing the wall.
The cunt crawled on top of the bed,
prodding my shoulder with its
spindly fingernails. I side-eyed the
twerp and spat out another
enquiry. The little sprite bowled
over again, giggling and hollering,
pissing itself basically. I flicked on a
a lamp and rubbed my sockets. The
imp held up my iPhone, showing
me hilarious videos and daft as fuck
memes. The pair of us spent dawn
keeled on our sides; in fits of
h   y   s   t   e   r   i   a.

THE AIRPORT.

I keep waking up on June 7th.

Each day the date stays the same.

I keep waking up on June 7th.

Each day the date stays the same.

I keep waking up on June 7th.

MONSTER.

     A shit monster. A monster made of shit, plopped his key in his front door. This shit monster was made up of all types of shit; dog shit, cat shit, bullshit, human shit. Bird shit. Horse shit. Shit TV, shit opinions, music that sounds like shit. Shitty little children, elephant shit (commonly known as dung), bat shit, the good shit, shih tzus, new shit, shiitake mushrooms, and shit I couldn't recognise. He wasn't a 'shit' monster, he was a very good monster as it turned out, on account of being head to toe covered in total shit. The shit monster slumped onto his sofa, scribbled away in his journal, and floated off to sleep.

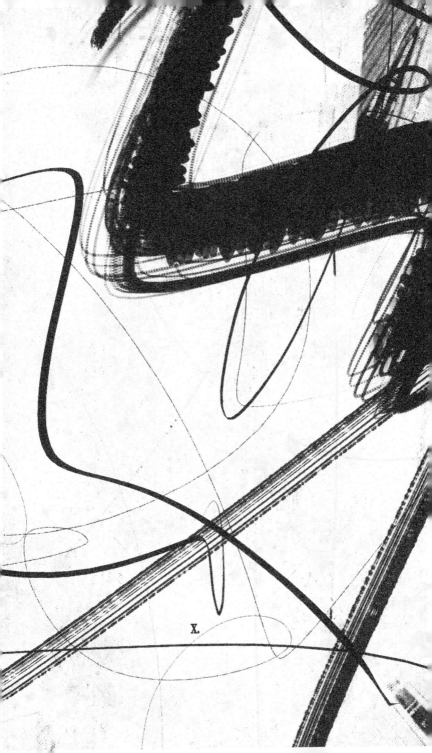

X.

THE HARBOUR.

Lily ran through the harbour, taking photos of the boats rocking under spotlights. The rattle of buoys bobbing was all that broke the silence. For a moment, Lily forgot the years of heartbreak and the love she no longer had left to give. Each evening, she could escape the pain she hadn't meant to cause. She could run to the harbour and home again. For now that's all Lily needed.

BANSHEE.

Before I could lift my foot from the ground, the phantom glided motionlessly towards me. I pounced and lobbed the spectre into the drum with the rest, loaded the machine with a quid, and put them on a delicate cycle. The laundrette lights flickered as the spooks whirled, moaning like banshees.

PACMAN.

Stepping off the train onto familiar platforms. Painful goodbyes and laughter lingered throughout this city in equal measure.

HERE LIES THE BODY
OF THE AUTHOR.

Out in the middle of fuck knows where, the author of the book *Fast Asleep In Terrapin Soup* barricades himself in a lighthouse. He turns away from his half-eaten udon noodles, pulling his quilt tight around his head. Occasionally, the author makes his way up to the beacon and watches over the ocean, wishing the great fish Namazu would bring it all crashing down. The author leans against the barriers of the beacon's viewing platform, wondering all his thoughts away, deep beneath the
w   a   v   e   s.

READY,
A B L E

THERAPY.

"Do you believe humans can harness magnetic abilities?" I asked, balancing somewhere between two to three spoons on the curves of my face. "That's our time up for this week," she responded.

A TOP MORNING.

Finally! Top hats are back in fashion. I sprang open my hat drawer and popped a top hat on top of my bonce. I waddled into the street, greeted by so much doffing. I doffed the milkman, and sure enough, he doffed me back. I strolled by my elderly neighbours, spun on my heel, and gave them a doff - they loved it! The greengrocer had a gargantuan top hat on top, that loomed all the way to the damn ceiling. He smirked and yanked a chain to his left, triggering a doffing mechanism that lifted the lid high off his nut. I doffed the hell outta him and gathered my apples.

BACK SEAT.

A hippo. A great big hippopotamus. Sitting on the back seats of the bus. This meathead was happy as Larry, resting his ginormous chomper and gazing out the window at all the passing cars. I paid my fare and gestured to the driver, "What's with this guy?" The driver skewed his head around to check out what I was referring to. "Don't mind him, he's with me." I approached the grey mass hesitantly; he didn't bat an eyelid. Parking myself by a window seat I scrolled through my phone and quickly forgot about the hippo; he was no trouble at all.

TOAST.

The toilet flushes, and the bathroom door slips shut. There's a commotion in the lounge. The smell of toast and cat food - either tuna or the brown sludgy one; they all smell the same. Claws clatter on the laminate. The cranes that once occupied the bedroom window now live behind my eyelids. You slouch back into bed with two wedges of toast, wiping crumbs into my hair. I wake up, and your buttered fingers vanish, claws turn back to rain.

THE SAD ALBUM.

I wrote the saddest sad album of all time. This sad fuck would go down in the history books. The opening track was about love. Another about some dead people followed right up it's arse. The middle section was mainly about sad things, like abandoned pets and charity shop wedding dresses. I wrote a slow one about looking at the sea. Everybody was so sad listening to my album. I spun the tunes on wax and considered changing a few things, y'know, like life stuff.

BOBBLEHEAD.

Antixera

caught me off guard. One false step into the danger zone and I was a goner. Suspended in the atmos, drifting like a plastic bag packed to the brim with fuckin' zilch. I scrambled in my pockets for my phone, firing out texts to anyone and everyone I knew had immediate access to a fishing rod or at least some type of decent net. "IT'S HAPPENED AGAIN!"

PANDA.

The panda went where I went, ate what I ate, watched what I watched, and slept where I slept. He'd join me at the gym and always come out for coffee. The panda would never leave my side. He'd sit on the toilet lid while I showered, and passed utensils while I cooked. We never said a word to each other; neither of us had anything at all to say. He was void of any colour, and so was I. Nobody else could see my panda, apart from maybe you? After all, he used to be yours.

TYRANNOSAUR.

One year of digging and dusting, fingernails laced with dirt. T h o u s a n d s of seemingly insignificant fossils placed to one side for further inspection. I climbed to the top of the scaffolding, struck by the scale of this excavation.

BOUNTY HUNTER.

The hunter sniffed around The Serpentine, knocking over deckchairs, bleeding cans of Stella, picking through seafood platters of shrimp and calamari. He skulked around Victoria Park, inspecting disused pizza boxes and half-eaten chicken burgers. Our trail took him to Bethnal Green, where he traced blades of broken grass and an abandoned wedding planner back to you and I. When you took west and I took south, the hunter lost our scent. We'd become strangers over time; we stood a b e t t e r c h a n c e a p a r t.

THIRTEEN SAUSAGES.

Five knights of the realm
ordered an English Breakfast
at a local greasy spoon: three Fully
Loaded's and two All Day
Breakfasts. Between them, there
were thirteen sausages, eight bacon
rashers, six fried eggs, and
two mounds of scramble. They
requested the baked beans be
placed in goblets in the middle of
the table. This place didn't have any
goblets lying around, though they
managed to source a couple of
ramekins. One of the knights
hesitantly enquired whether his
grilled tomatoes could be swapped
for extra mushrooms. Ten hash
browns, four black puddings, and
essentially two entire loaves of
toasted bread. The knights
struggled to open their portions of
Anchor butter through their
gauntlets. A waitress assisted in
buttering their toast while they sat
patiently. The scent of ketchup and
HP Brown Sauce billowed to the
clinks and clanks of these five
knights as they tucked into their
hearty breakfasts.

HELTER SKELTER.

She was wearing stilts - bold move for a first date. I could barely get a good look at her as she soared past nearby office blocks. I howled at the top of my lungs, whether she fancied a coffee on the way to the pier? Not even a peek. She was making Goliath strides while I ran alongside, weaving between her mighty pins. I clung to her masts as she catapulted toward the coast. I scampered to the top of the Helter Skelter as she waded out to sea. We chatted for hours about what she did for work and where she grew up. I was required to whizz back down to the bottom every fifteen minutes to let tourists pass, which really was fair enough.

TOTAL ECLIPSE.

Jaffa Cakes brought back that advert about the moons. This time, they included every possible incarnation, from the waxing gibbous to the waning crescent. They dove into different types of eclipses and its phases, according to airtight astrology. A few former dregs from NASA were employed to provide expert supervision, and the entire project was filmed on the international space station. The advert took years to produce and cost millions. Thankfully, they didn't change the recipe, and Jaffa Cakes are still tasty as fuck.

SUGARLAND.

Everything started to taste a little sweeter. There was a vibrancy to everything that I hadn't noticed in a while. I chomped into a nearby chocolate oak tree and nibbled at the ticket inspector's Parma violet nose. I pierced my gnashers into my own forearm, causing a gruesome fountain of blood to drench nearby liquorice spectators and a sherbet hound. Tendons and arteries wriggling like non-gummy gummy worms. Though I wasn't part of this sugarland, I was interested to see how far it went.

BLOOM.

Flowers had faces, with little eyes and mouths and frown lines. Some of them grew arms and legs, embraced, and fell in love.

DAFFY.

Daffy burnt the feathers and skin clean off his arse. Ten superb somersaults landed him rectum-first into a bucket of ice. Daffy turned his quivering bill towards me, sitting on a tree stump writing this book about you. He rolled up his sleeves, began marching over, and slammed the bucket over my head. Oh, brother.

ESPIONAGE.

What are you doing? Are you watching TV? Dancing to one of your playlists? Or one of our playlists? Are you drinking a beer in your pants? Or sharing a bottle of wine on a date? Are you fighting a cold? Maybe you're wrapped up in the spare duvet on the sofa, feeling sorry for yourself with a LemSip. Did you think about me today? Did that make you happy or sad? Indifferent, maybe. Are you making that curry we made three nights in a row? Or have you not made that since, either? Are you planning a holiday? I wonder where to? Somewhere on our list? Maybe Lisbon? Are you wondering what I'm doing? What I'm wearing today. Whether or not I'm still thinking about you? Are you working at the same place? If you are, are you working from bed or did you ever buy a desk? Are you seeing the same friends or new ones? Are you decorating? Are you using the paint I bought for the bedroom? Are you trying on a new dress for the weekend, or doing yoga after the weekend just gone?

Are you reading a new book? Or the letter I sent? I wonder if you ever picked up that floristry class again? Are you still turning pages over in the calendar on the wall, or is that one reminder too many? The months are racking up now. Are you at a gig or taking it easy this month? I bought two tickets the other day out of habit. Are you healthy? Are you working through those boxes? I guess what I really want to know is, do you ever miss me this much?

FLOATER.

A toad floated in through my bedroom window. I'd never seen a toad so distressed. He meandered through the room, setting my books and curtains ablaze. The toad found himself bobbing about above the door frame. I unlocked its prison, and the breeze sent him drifting down the staircase, knocking down cherished family portraits and igniting the rest of the house.

ARCHIPELAGO.

All the intricate details that made me, me, were written out on Post-it notes and stuck up on the mirror. My kindness, my insecurities, my love of breakfast foods - everything was up there. My GCSE results, my sexual fantasies, my swimming badges, and all my P45s. The way I worry when I let someone down and every single shopping list. All the nightmares that follow me and the things that make me blush. Texts I regret, times I've wanted to die, and the three times I had tried. Notes describing how deeply I've loved. Riding a bike wasn't on there because I never learned. There was a Post-it note that read 'can't ride a bike' though, just underneath 'never made lasagne.'

ANOTHER DAY.

Dappling light and tendrils bounce across the wall. My phone, facedown on my chest. I know there's no chance in this life that I'll hear from you. Not today, not tomorrow, but it sits on my chest and I wait anyway. I wait like I did yesterday, like I did a year ago today, because today is just another day. Like all the rest.

BUGEYE.

Now we were getting
somewhere. Two slaps on the elbow
meant *hello,* three flicks on the
belly meant *next question.* Running
on the spot was its way of laughing.
This alien turned out to be world-
class company. I learned its
language fast and told it all about
Earth. I told it all about you. It
collected me in its slimy pincers
and drooled gunge over my head,
which was its way of saying:
"Y o u ' r e   g o n n a   b e
j   u   s   t   f   i   n   e."

PRONGS.

It was raining starfish - hundreds upon thousands of the five-pronged fuckers hailing from the sky, smackin' the pavement with a satisfying squelch. Folk sheltered in nearby cafès and under beach chalets. I was loving this. A starfish perched on my shoulder, another trickling down the back of my shirt. I strolled past a chap sprawled flat on the ground, absolutely drenched in the stuff. Taking up residence on a bench overlooking the ocean, I watched all the lucky starfish for miles landing in the drink. I rummaged around in my jacket pocket and pulled out a Snickers bar. I was absolutely loving this.

KIMCHI.

I   l o v e   y o u.

It ferments inside my chest, the
meaning adjusts each day. But the
truth of it is, it's still I love you,
it   will   always   be

I   l o v e   y o u.

PAPER LANTERNS.

Outcasts and oddballs gathered in the centre of town. Monkey gods and radish men, raccoons clad in tracksuits and onion mobsters smokin' cigarillos. Glowing bulbs of fireflies illuminated pathways, origami platypus operating food trucks spread the scent of terrapin soup throughout the band of misfits. I budged between the lady with one hundred eyes and her husband formed of fungus. The townsfolk lit their lanterns and painted the sky in dragon fire. The evening succumbed to its unparalleled beauty; it was here where I let you go.

POACHED EGGS.

Sunday afternoon at the bottom of a well. There's a stranger down here with me, yapping away about her favourite films and the ideal roast dinner. Getting out the well didn't seem as urgent to this acquaintance of mine; she'd been here a bit longer. She told me she was looking forward to getting out and enjoying the sunshine again. She managed to convince me we'd come up with a plan in our own time. For now, it was nice just chatting away. I eased into the idea of the well and asked about her favourite holiday destination.

MAGPIE.

"This is all my stuff"
I said, gesturing around the room. I
had all sorts in here: my vinyl
collection, multiple breeds of
houseplants, a *Brouwerij't ij
Amsterdam* beer mat, pebbles from
Brighton beach, a broken vintage
Canon film camera with three
detachable lenses, various prints
and paintings adorning the walls,
and the twelve month payment
plan on my cord two-seater futon. I
flopped down on my linen sheets as
she flicked through sketchbooks
and notepads piled next to my bed.
"Who's this?" She asked, nodding
towards scribbles of a girl in a
hospital gown. Her finger stalled,
absorbing the unsent letters and
journal entires from a time not long
ago. She flopped backward on the
linen. "So, this is all your stuff?" I
tapped her thigh with a drumstick
and asked if she wanted to dance.

THE END OF THE WORLD.

I walked all the way to the end of the world. Alabaster cliffs, abundant in moss, soaring far into the cerulean. The tide was still, the sun shone bright, and life was slower here. I could stay here, at the end of the world, in total isolation, where nobody could find me. But who really wants that? I gathered my belongings and began the punishing rise up the cliff side. It was time to come home.

MINT CHOC CHIP.

Tucking into a bowl of gelato, his shell resting against the rocky walls of his aquarium, Grayson felt Lily's presence. He sat with her beside him, not moving a muscle, not a word or a glance. He wondered if she could feel him too, wherever she was. There was so much Grayson wanted to tell her, but for now he was content, sitting with his memories, scooping away at s o m e   m i n t   c h o c   c h i p.

PEACHES.

We were bruised, but never rotten.
This will be how I remember
you.

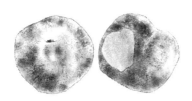

ACKNOWLEDGEMENTS.

Who, without whom, this book would have been unbearable.

SAM GRANT | MARK KISZELY
HANNAH PARKES
ANDREW SKINNER-SHAH
AMY BAKER
PAULA ROELAS
CHANI MERRELL
CLARE O'HAGAN
MARTINA MCLOUGHLIN
LEWIS SPENCER

Printed in Great Britain
by Amazon

58785049R00083